1 Introduction

Country context: Ethiopia

Despite enjoying considerable economic growth in recent years, Ethiopia is still struggling with the impacts of civil war and protracted humanitarian emergencies, including the ongoing armed conflict between government and Tigrayan forces that began in November 2020. Against a backdrop of insecurity, political instability and periodic famine, the country's education and health systems remain underdeveloped, with limited funding and many inequalities.

The challenges are especially acute for the nation's minorities and indigenous peoples. An ethnically and linguistically diverse country, with more than 90 distinct ethnic groups and almost as many languages, in principle Ethiopia's federalist structure and clear constitutional recognition of minority rights guarantee a significant amount of regional autonomy.[1] Ethiopia's 11 states have different ethnic compositions: for example, Oromia, Amhara, Tigray and Somali are primarily inhabited by the four largest ethnic groups, namely Oromo (34.5 per cent), Amhara (26.9 per cent), Somali (6.2 per cent) and Tigray (6.1 per cent).[2] Yet in reality, the political mobilization of identity and the dominance of particular communities and regions has led to acute inequalities and rising tensions between different groups. This has culminated in the civil conflict that, at the time of writing, showed little sign of abating and has now spread out from Tigray into other regions.

Focus of this briefing

In addition to increasing inter-ethnic tensions in recent years, reflected in a succession of protests and violent crackdowns, pronounced inequalities exist between different regions, with strong communal dimensions. These are especially evident in terms of education and health services. Despite significant progress in both areas at the national level, many of these benefits remain out of reach for a large proportion of minority and indigenous community members. This briefing presents a selection of relevant indicators to highlight these regional divisions.

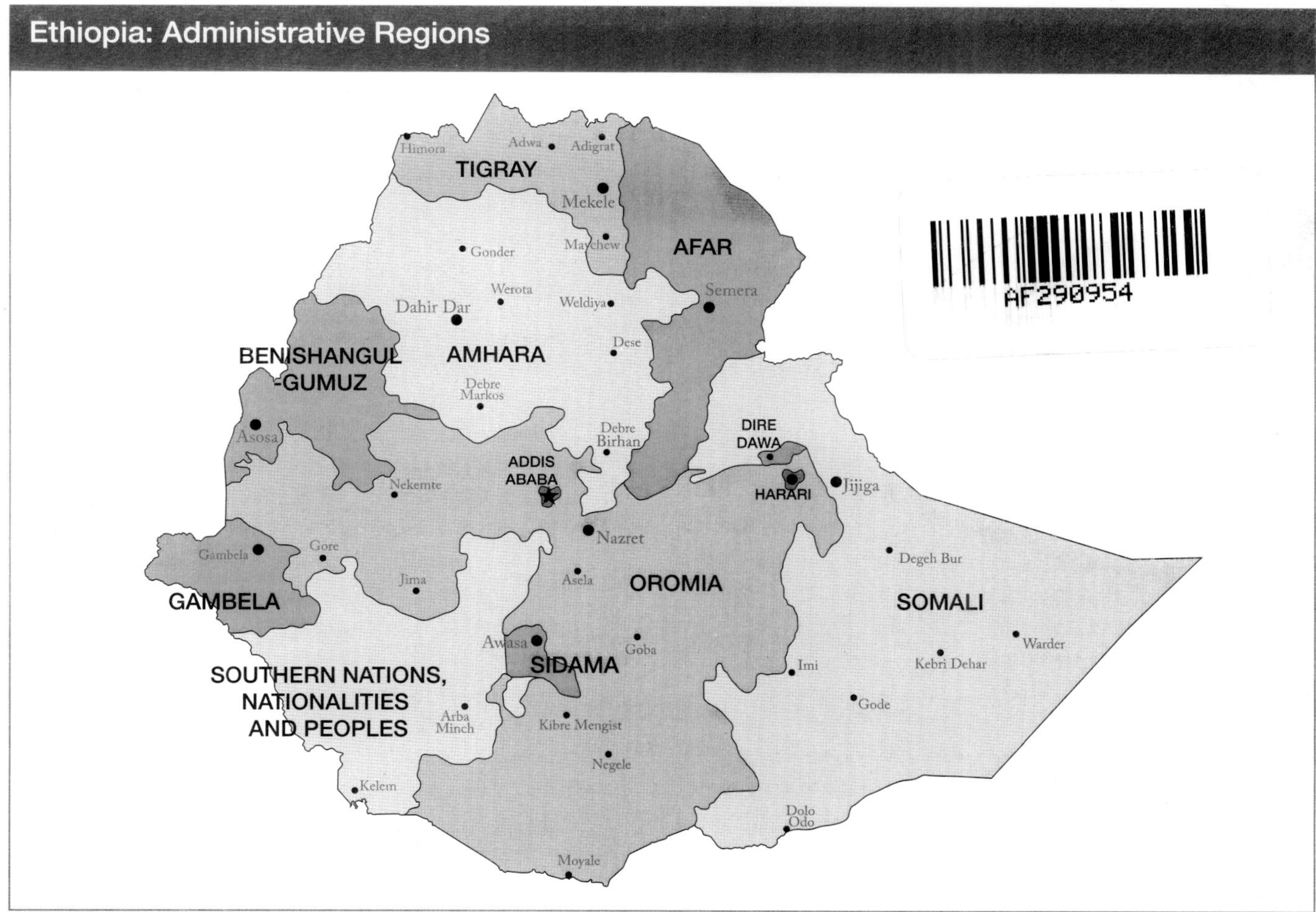

3

2 Education

Policy and funding

While educational funding is split between the regional and federal governments, with the latter providing between 50 and 60 per cent of the funding, the country's education programme is highly centralized: the Ministry of Education largely determines admissions, enrolments and curricula, even at the level of higher education, with university staff frequently appointed on the basis of their politics rather than academic credentials. Nevertheless, elementary school education is conducted in a number of different languages, varying from region to region, including Amharic, Oromo, Somali, Tigrinya and at least 10 other languages, before English is used as the main medium of instruction from grade five onwards.[3]

Ethiopia's most recent policy framework on education, the *Education Sector Development Programme V (2015/16–2019/20)* (henceforth *ESDP V*),[4] outlines a range of objectives around increased attainment and equitable access in line with the Sustainable Development Goals. Among other areas, *ESDP V* acknowledges the need to attract teachers to 'remote and ethnic minority areas' through incentives, and other measures to improve attendance, including food ration packages for schoolgirls from pastoralist communities. Other measures include commitments to provide solar-powered tablets, given the absence of electricity networks in some rural areas, and the upgrading of 40 per cent of Alternative Basic Education centres into formal primary schools. These will also be supported by the creation of mobile school units and the establishment of boarding houses for hard-to-reach pastoralist children. It also identifies pastoralist children as one of several priority groups to be engaged through community awareness raising and mobilization efforts, further aided by the establishment of a National Council for Pastoralist Education to support the development and management of recruitment, facilities, nutrition and sanitation.

The 2008 Pastoralist Area Education Strategy was developed with the specific aim of expanding access to pastoralist communities and of closing the gap in educational attainment between pastoralist communities and the rest of the country. Its provisions include the creation of an Alternative Basic Education (ABE) programme and the development of low-cost schools, mobile schools and boarding houses, as well as the use of existing Qur'anic schools in villages as places of instruction for the secular ABE programme. It also outlines a range of measures to address the economic, cultural and environmental barriers to attendance, with initiatives including free school meals, gender-segregated sanitation facilities and community engagement.

Ethiopia has also implemented measures to expand educational access to children with disabilities, who face greater barriers to accessing school and attend in lower numbers. For instance, the 2012–21 National Plan of Action of Persons with Disabilities outlines a strategy to increase inclusion in a range of areas, including education, through expanded facilities and trained staff to cater to special needs. However, significant disparities in access still persist.[5] The Special Needs/Inclusive Education Strategy was published in 2012, developed to replace an earlier iteration from 2006 following Ethiopia's ratification of the United Nations (UN) Convention on the Rights of Persons with Disabilities in 2010.

With 56.8 million birr of federal funding earmarked for education in FY 2020/21, the sector enjoyed the second largest allocation in the country, after roads.[6] It is worth noting that, with a large part of the country's education funding deriving from international sources, at some points surplus budget has gone unspent. For example, in FY 2016/17, the federal education budget credibility was 107 – a situation that may reflect unpredictable aid flows and limited absorptive capacity within the government to effectively disburse the funds.[7]

Achievements and challenges

Ethiopia's educational outcomes have improved significantly in recent years, with primary school enrolment more than doubling during the Millennium Development Goal (MDG) period, from 40.2 per cent in 2000 to 84.6 per cent in 2015.[8] Net secondary school enrolment remains significantly lower, though the country has seen similar improvements in recent years, rising from 12.5 per cent in 2000 to 30.8 per cent in 2015.[9] During this period, the gender disparities in educational access have also narrowed, though considerable gaps remain: for example, male and female net primary school enrolment rates were 87.7 per cent and 81.4 per cent in 2015, compared to 46.0 per cent and 34.2 per cent in 2000.[10] These improvements have been driven by significant government investment, with the number of qualified teachers in the general education system almost doubling from 323,695 in 2013/14 to 620,654 in 2017/18.[11] Similarly, at the tertiary level, the gross rate of enrolment of students has increased dramatically, from around 1.2 per cent in 2000 to 9.6 per cent in 2015,[12] though here too gender inequalities are also evident with male enrolment (12.3 per cent) markedly higher than female (6.8 per cent).[13]

Regional inequalities

Despite these impressive numbers, Ethiopia's educational progress has been put in doubt in light of the ongoing challenges it faces, from financial pressures to a decline in the quality of instruction. Among other shortcomings, adult illiteracy remains persistently high, as do levels of school drop-out, and inequalities in educational outcomes in relation to gender, income and location are sharp – in particular, between urban and rural areas. Given that more than half of youth do not complete their primary education, in addition to those who never secure any formal education, the true picture of educational attainment appears more mixed. As for tertiary education, a lack of trained teaching staff, limited equipment and poor infrastructure have also contributed to a university setting that is simultaneously elitist and poorly performing, ranking below many other countries in the East Africa region.[14]

Millions of Ethiopian children are out of school, amounting to 14.4 per cent of the primary school age population as of 2015: 911,879 boys and 1,394,680 girls.[15] Poverty, geographical distance and the fact that many children work or are responsible for household chores all contribute to this shortfall. Furthermore, because of traditional gender norms and expectations, many girls in particular are unable to attend school. The large numbers of displaced and refugee children in Ethiopia also face additional barriers to accessing education. UNICEF operates programmes to provide education to children in these challenging humanitarian contexts.

Barriers for pastoralists and minorities

There are serious challenges around reaching remote and marginalized groups, especially pastoralists, who collectively make up between 12 and 15 million people in the country, with most located in the regions of Afar, Somali, the South Omo Zone in the Southern Nations, Nationalities and Peoples' Region (SNNPR), and Borena Zone in Oromia. The lack of even basic infrastructure in these areas, as well as the challenges relating to the year-round migration that is an integral part of the pastoralists' livelihood, is further complicated by the increasingly unpredictable weather patterns brought by climate change. This is reflected in their significantly lower uptake of primary school education.[16] The government has responded with a number of initiatives, such as the previously mentioned ABE programme, mobile schools and distance learning, to provide more accessible and appropriate educational services to these communities. For instance, school timings have been designed to be more flexible to accommodate seasonal migration and traditional livelihoods, with efforts focused on ensuring a high-quality education is available and comprehensible through local-language content and gender-sensitive measures to increase the participation of pastoralist girls in formal education.[17]

The disparities are even more stark when data is disaggregated by region and gender. Looking at female educational attainment in the 15–49-years age range, the Somali region scored worst, with 75.3 per cent having no education, followed by Afar region at 68.7 per cent. These are the two regions where the majority of pastoralist communities reside. By comparison, other regions fare significantly better, with the lowest rates reported in Addis Ababa (8.6 per cent) and the next lowest by Gambela (26.7 per cent).

Regarding literacy levels, again Afar and Somali regions both perform very poorly. For instance, only 1.2 per cent of the 15–49-year-old female population in both regions have gone through more than secondary education. Improving this necessitates the targeted expansion of secondary and higher education in areas of the country where access is currently very limited.

Table 1: Selected educational attainment indicators among women aged 15–49, by region (%)

Region	No education	Primary school attendance rate	More than a secondary education
Tigray	43.0	83.2	2.7
Afar	68.7	62.0	1.2
Amhara	54.1	78.6	2.0
Oromiya	51.1	66.1	1.4
Somali	75.3	56.2	1.2
Benishangul-Gumuz	46.7	71.0	1.6
SNNPR	43.9	73.3	1.5
Gambela	26.7	89.1	3.2
Harari	36.1	72.5	4.2
Addis Adaba	8.6	85.1	13.7
Dire Dawa	33.3	71.5	3.4

Source: Ethiopian Demographic and Health Survey (EDHS), 2016. *Note*: Sidama region does not appear in the list because the data was gathered before its formation in 2020.

As for levels of school attendance, Somali and Afar regions scored poorly, with net female attendance rates of 56.2 per cent and 62.0 per cent respectively. Various social and economic reasons may be at play here: limited security, a lack of stable, well-functioning schools in remote areas, and financial barriers that prevent families sending their children to school. A huge amount of work is therefore needed to close this gap.

Access to education among children with disabilities

The exact number of persons with disabilities in Ethiopia is uncertain. Figures from the 1994 national census estimated that around 991,916 people, amounting to 1.8 per cent of the national population at the time, had disabilities.[18] However, this is far lower than other projections: for example, according to UNICEF, extrapolating from 2015/16 survey data, almost 7.8 million people in the country had disabilities – around 9.3 per cent of the total population at the time. Of these, around 2.2 million people had very severe disabilities. Most prevalence appears to be concentrated among older groups, with around 1 per cent of those under 18 having severe disability compared to around 13 per cent in those aged over 60. However, the true incidence of severe disability among children may be higher due to under-reporting and data collection challenges.[19]

Despite some improvements in recent years, the challenges that children with disabilities face in accessing education are illustrated by 2015–16 household survey data that showed that 43 per cent of children with disabilities had never attended school, compared to a national average of 22 per cent.[20] Previous studies have highlighted the very small proportion of children with disabilities who have been able to enjoy a quality education, especially outside urban areas, and the limited recognition and resources given to cater for their specific needs in mainstream schools – a situation that has likely contributed to their high drop-out rate.[21] Handicap International has estimated that as few as 3 per cent of children with disabilities in Ethiopia attend school.[22] Stigma and discrimination serve as additional barriers. Consequently, there is a pressing need for more specialist training, tailored educational tools and holistic support in the form of health facilities, financial support and awareness raising.

3 Health services

Policy and funding

In line with its fiscal decentralization strategy, an increasing proportion of health spending is now undertaken at the regional level, rising from 61.5 per cent in 2012/13 to 70.3 per cent in 2016/17. At the same time, a significant amount of funding is channelled from external sources, with 71 per cent of federal capital health expenditure in 2016/17 coming from development partners. Nevertheless, despite nominal spending levels on health rising substantially, in real terms annual per capita expenditure declined slightly from 216 birr[23] in 2012/13 to 212 birr in 2016/17 – in the process placing pressure on households to meet the gap themselves. Data from 2016/17 shows that 31 per cent of health expenditure was in the form of out-of-pocket spending, a level that indicates 'catastrophic health expenditure levels'.[24]

In this context, for poor and marginalized communities the barriers to access can be particularly acute, notwithstanding efforts to support inclusive coverage through measures such as the Community-Based Health Insurance programme, designed to reach informal sector workers and impoverished rural communities. Besides the financial challenges, accessing adequate infrastructure and trained personnel in remote areas can be very difficult. With around one physician per 13,000 people as of 2018,[25] medical resources are already stretched at a national level, but these pressures become even starker in certain regions where even private health services are extremely difficult to come by.

Achievements and challenges

While Ethiopia's health system has struggled for decades, in recent years it has seen significant improvement, with the country achieving many of its targets under the MDGs, including a significant reduction in maternal mortality rates and the number of deaths from diseases such as HIV/AIDS, malaria and tuberculosis.[26] Yet this significant progress at a national level has not been distributed equitably, with minorities and marginalized communities in many remote and hard-to-reach areas still unable to access regular health services, a situation made worse by insecurity and the ongoing conflict in the north of the country. This is reflected in the Ethiopian Demographic and Health Survey (EDHS) data that shows clear disparities between health outcomes in those regions where most of the country's pastoralist and minority populations are concentrated.[27]

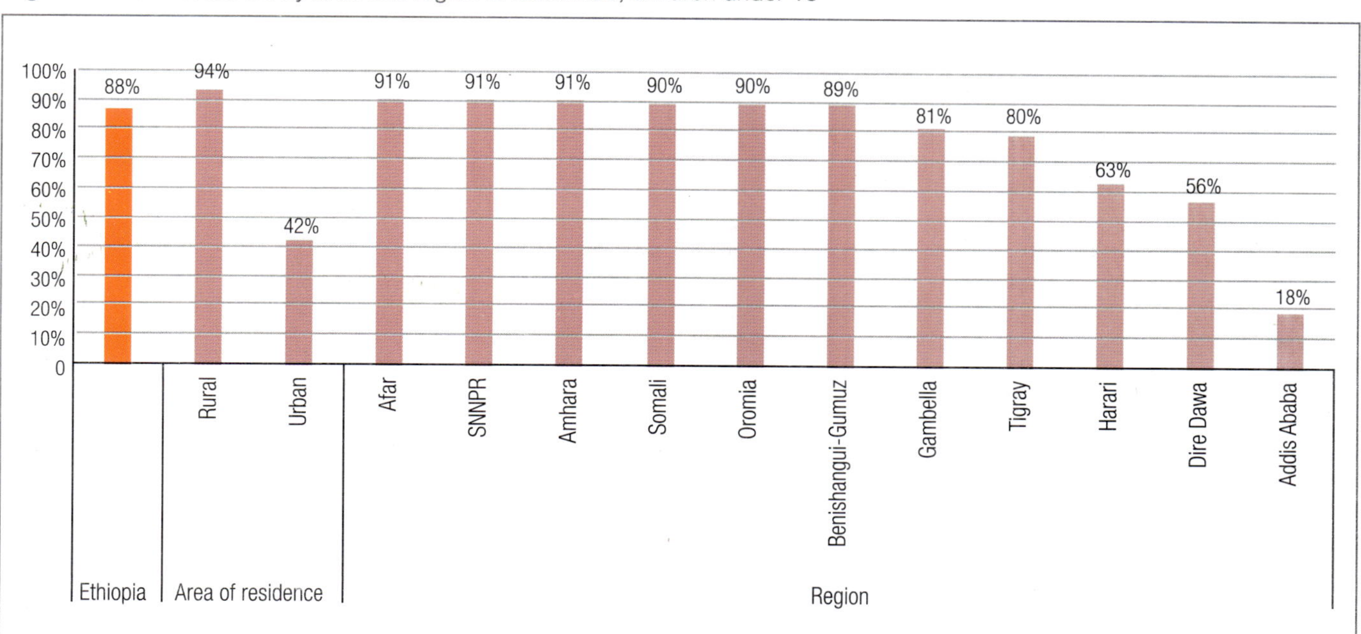

Figure 1: MCD incidence by area and region of residence, children under 18

Source: Central Statistical Agency and UNICEF Ethiopia, Multidimensional Child Deprivation in Ethiopia, Addis Ababa, 2018, based on the EDHS 2016 data.
Note: Sidama region does not appear in the list because the data was gathered before its formation in 2020.

Barriers for pastoralists and minorities

Looking at the breakdown of multidimensional child deprivation (MCD) by region, for example, the gaps between urban (42 per cent) and rural (94 per cent) areas, and between Addis Ababa (18 per cent) and regions such as Afar (91 per cent), SNNPR (91 per cent), Somali (90 per cent) and Oromia (90 per cent) illustrate the uneven health outcomes across the country.[28] In those areas where pastoralists and other marginalized communities are concentrated, childhood deprivation is the norm rather than the exception.

While Ethiopia may have met the maternal health goals of the MDGs at a national level, poor outcomes are still evident among minority communities in Ethiopia, particularly pastoralist and nomadic societies. For instance, only 43.6 per cent of Somali mothers have received ante-natal care from skilled personnel, meaning the remainder have either not received ante-natal care at all or were attended by non-professionals. The figure is even higher in Oromia, where almost half of the mothers (48.6 per cent) have not received any ante-natal care at all. Similarly, in terms of access to institutional delivery, fewer than a quarter (23.3 per cent) of births in Somali region take place in a health facility.

Table 2: Selected health indicators by region, 2016

Region	No ante-natal care (%)	Births in a health facility (%)	Under-5 mortality rates (per 1,000 live births)	Children 12– 23 months old with all basic vaccines (%)	Percentage of women circumcized
Tigray	43.0	83.2	2.7	43.0	83.2
Afar	68.7	62.0	1.2	68.7	62.0
Amhara	54.1	78.6	2.0	54.1	78.6
Oromiya	51.1	66.1	1.4	51.1	66.1
Somali	75.3	56.2	1.2	75.3	56.2
Benishangul-Gumuz	46.7	71.0	1.6	46.7	71.0
SNNPR	43.9	73.3	1.5	43.9	73.3
Gambela	26.7	89.1	3.2	26.7	89.1
Harari	36.1	72.5	4.2	36.1	72.5
Addis Adaba	8.6	85.1	13.7	8.6	85.1
Dire Dawa	33.3	71.5	3.4	33.3	71.5

Source: EDHS, 2016. *Note*: Sidama region does not appear in the list because the data was gathered before its formation in 2020.

These shortfalls translate into high levels of child mortality. Despite the reduction in overall child mortality in Ethiopia in recent years, levels remain high and are particularly elevated in Afar, where the under-5 mortality rate is at 125 per 1,000 live births. Given that one of the most serious causes of child mortality is lack of access to vaccines, immunization coverage is an important and related area where, again, regional disparities are evident. The proportion of infants who have received all basic vaccines is lowest in Afar (15.2 per cent), Somali (21.8 per cent) and Oromia (24.7 per cent). This does not bode well for the ability of the country's Covid-19 vaccination programme to reach pastoralist communities, especially when vaccination levels at a national level are still low.

Besides increasing the risk of prolonged labour – a major cause of maternal mortality – female circumcision leads to a variety of other lifelong health issues. Though widespread across the country, the prevalence of female circumcision is especially high in Somali (98.5 per cent) and Afar (91.2 per cent) regions. When disaggregated directly by ethnicity, the prevalence in some communities is even clearer, with the highest levels among Somali (98.5 per cent), Afar (98.4 per cent), Hadiya (92.3 per cent) and Welaita (92.3 per cent) Ethiopians.[29]

Access to health care among persons with disabilities

Health challenges may be especially acute among persons with disabilities, who may face even greater hurdles to securing mainstream services due to social marginalization, not to mention securing more specialized care to assist them in managing their conditions. For example, it has been reported that young persons with disabilities often have limited awareness around sexual and reproductive health: the government should focus efforts on ensuring engagement with these groups, and that they have access to information.[30] National health policies still have only a limited focus on disability as a specific priority, with non-governmental organizations still providing much of the tailored health and social care to persons with disabilities.[31]

4 Conclusion and recommendations

Despite Ethiopia's significant progress in education and health in recent years, significant gaps remain. This is especially evident at the regional level, with those areas largely inhabited by pastoralists and other minorities typically facing some of the worst outcomes. This highlights, first of all, the importance of more disaggregated data to specifically identify educational attainment and health outcomes among ethnic and religious minorities and indigenous peoples, as well as persons with disabilities. There also needs to be more research on the specific intersectional challenges experienced by persons with disabilities belonging to marginalized communities.

Addressing the complex mix of social exclusion, stigma, poverty, geographical factors and institutional failure that contribute to the difficulties these different groups face in accessing basic services requires a multidimensional, holistic response. Authorities must therefore build on their existing efforts to deliver accessible, culturally appropriate education and health care through targeted investments and transformative policies that seek to address the root causes of the continued marginalization of these groups in Ethiopian society.

Addressing these shortfalls and inequalities is all the more important in the midst of the current conflict and the ongoing effects of the Covid-19 pandemic. It is vital that every effort is made to ensure that education, health and other services are maintained in the face of these challenges, and in particular that specific regions are not disadvantaged or prioritized by the national government.

Recommendations

To the Government of Ethiopia:

Focus on enhancing the collection and management of disaggregated education and health data: Identifying and responding to disparities in service access and quality is essential to the promotion of equitable education and health systems. Clear, reliable data that is disaggregated by gender, ethnicity, religion, age, geographical location and disability status is a central element in achieving this. For example, while the 2016 Ethiopian Demographic and Health Survey includes ethnicity and religion as specific variables in a number of its published datasets (primarily around the prevalence of female genital mutilation (FGM) and gender-based violence), much of the information it presents is only disaggregated by region. Although this provides a useful proxy for minority and indigenous

outcomes, it nevertheless frames these differences as to do with geographical location rather than a reflection of communal inequalities.

Ensure education and health services are delivered in a culturally appropriate fashion to minorities, indigenous peoples and persons with disabilities: There is a need for tailored and accessible service provision for communities such as pastoralists who may face significant barriers to securing education and health care through standardized systems. Commendably, this is already reflected in some official policies, but significant gaps remain. First and foremost, authorities at all levels must actively engage minority and indigenous communities to provide them with the opportunity to participate meaningfully in the design and development of local education and health services in order to maximize uptake, inclusion and accessibility. Particular attention must be paid to ensuring that marginalized voices, including women, older people and persons with disabilities within these communities, also have a say in the design of these services.

Target investments to ensure adequate services in remote and under-served areas, with a focus on quality as well as overall coverage: Ethiopia's significant achievements during the Millennium Development Goals period (2000–15) nevertheless conceal ongoing gaps that, in line with the commitment of the Sustainable Development Goals to 'leave no one behind', should be addressed through additional spending to resolve the shortages of education and health infrastructure and personnel. In particular, given their growing importance and widespread unavailability in some regions of the country, the provision of ICT facilities and training should be a priority when investing in education to serve minority and indigenous communities.

Incorporate humanitarian and environmental concerns: Disasters, drought, locust swarms, and other extreme water and food shortages all have the potential to disrupt regular education and health services, particularly for pastoralist communities. The outbreak of civil war in parts of the country has exacerbated this insecurity and poses a major risk to service access, as well as the safety and wellbeing of populations in conflict-affected areas. Addressing this will require robust, regular assessments and enhanced coordination between government providers and partners. International donors should also work together to expand funding for emergency education and health services in the current context.

Strengthen budgeting processes to ensure predictable, transparent spending for health care and other services: Given the government's dependence on international donor assistance to fund many essential services, there is a need to focus on improving efficiency and evaluation of expenditures to ensure future financial resilience, especially in a context where many donor countries are scaling back their development aid. Alongside this, authorities should do more to promote supplementary and informal support services, such as health insurance and social protection programmes, to mitigate the risks of overstretched or suspended service provision.